Original title:
Ice Ice Baby, Not So Nice

Copyright © 2024 Creative Arts Management OÜ
All rights reserved.

Author: Juliana Wentworth
ISBN HARDBACK: 978-9916-94-320-5
ISBN PAPERBACK: 978-9916-94-321-2

Frosty Remnants

Little flakes are falling down,
They land with an icy frown.
Slipped and slid on frozen ground,
A winter circus all around.

Snowmen grinning, hats askew,
One just fell! Oh what a view!
Hot cocoa warms my chilly hands,
But outside, chaos still stands.

The Ice That Hides

Beneath your feet, a shiny trap,
One wrong step and it's a slap!
With every slide, the laughter grows,
Watch your step, as ice bestows.

Puppies prance, they twist and spin,
Chasing snowballs, gleeful din.
Yet here I stand, a statue bold,
With ice skates on, feeling cold!

A Symphony of Shatter

Hear that crack? It's not a joke,
It's my dignity, about to choke.
As I dance with frosty grace,
Back to the ground, I find my place.

Chimes of laughter fill the air,
With every tumble, without a care.
My friends all cheer, then lose their way,
A waltz on ice gone slightly gray.

Winter's Unwelcoming Hold

The door won't budge, it's stuck in freeze,
  Wrapping me up, like a frozen tease.
  With mittens thick, I give a shove,
  The world outside is cold, not love.

  Snowball fights turn into brawls,
  Everyone slips and down they fall.
  Shake it off, my shivering friends,
  This winter's grasp just never ends!

Shivers of the Past

Remember last winter when I hit the ground?
My dignity lost, but laughter was found.
That slip on the sidewalk, a sight to behold,
I danced like a penguin, feeling so bold.

Hot cocoa in hand, who needs a hot bath?
When snowflakes all giggle at my frosty path.
A tumble so grand, with a snowman's embrace,
I stood up with style, a smile on my face.

The Coldest Confession

I confessed my true love to the frosty air,
It chuckled and whispered, 'You're quite unaware.'
My heart was all frozen, like a popsicle sweet,
That chill in the breeze, it swept me off my feet.

With every bold word, my teeth chattered loud,
The snowflakes burst into a giggling crowd.
So I wrapped my warm heart in a thick woolen hug,
And sent my affection on a cold breezy tug.

Snowbound Secrets

Whispers of secrets buried deep in the snow,
Where the squirrels dance wildly, and nobody knows.
The snowman is guarding all things that we hide,
Like the time I fell flat, oh what a wild ride!

Oh, the sledding adventures that turned into fights,
I launched off the hill, oh what a sight!
Landing in piles of fluffy white fluff,
My laughter erupted, that just felt good stuff.

Slips and Falls

Watch where you're walking, the ground looks so fine,
'Til you find yourself flying like you're on a vine.
A graceful dismount, well that's just a joke,
With flailing and tumbling, I looked like a bloke.

We all share a laugh when our shoes get too slick,
The ice plays a trick, oh what a cruel lick!
Then we gather together, and share all the tales,
Of slips, falls, and giggles, amidst wintery gales.

Beneath a Layer of Cold

In the freezer of my heart, a chill does roam,
Where snowflakes laugh and icebergs call it home.
With frosty puns that tickle on my skin,
I bite my tongue, no warmth to be found within.

My coffee froze, it's blistering outside,
A snowman's grin, while I choose to hide.
The winter's quirks tickle my funny bone,
As laughter echoes through this icy zone.

Frigid Requiem

A winter tune played by a snowman's hat,
He dances about, and I fall flat.
With every slip, I'm a sight to behold,
The symphony plays, while the temp turns cold.

Frosty toes, and my fingers are numb,
This cold weather makes me feel so dumb.
Sipping on soup that's turned to a cube,
In this frozen realm, I find my own lube.

Heartstrings in a Snowstorm

Through flurries of frost, my heart beats loud,
It's hard to stay warm under this fluffy shroud.
I chase my dreams, but they're lost in the snow,
Each step's a slip, putting on quite a show.

A snowflake lands on my head like a crown,
I'm the royal jester in this frozen town.
With every laugh, my heart starts to thaw,
Underneath the chilly air, there's still some awe.

The Bitter Touch of Winter

Frosty kisses fall from the clouds above,
Though they sting a bit, I still feel love.
Snowball fights breaking out in the street,
Each icy attack makes me laugh on my feet.

My mittens dance, they itch and they poke,
While snowflakes fall like a silly joke.
The chill's got a grip, but I'll find the heat,
With laughter and warmth, this winter can't defeat.

Chilled to the Bone

I slipped on the ice, oh what a sight,
Fell like a penguin, with all my might.
The dog laughed so hard, he rolled on the ground,
While I lay like a snowman, totally sound.

The winter coat's thick, a small price to pay,
But overheated and sweating, oh what a day!
Sipping hot cocoa, the mug's in my hand,
Wishing for summer, a beach, and some sand.

When the Frost Leaves a Mark

Frostbite nipped at my toes with glee,
I danced in my boots but fell on my knee.
Snowflakes like cousins fell from the sky,
While I tried to catch one, oh me, oh my!

The snowman looked smug, it can't be denied,
While I stand beside him, my ego a slide.
His carrot nose winked, his eyes made of coal,
Shining bright like my one frozen soul.

The Bitter Frost of Truth

You think winter's a wonder, all glimmer and gold,
Till the truth sneaks up, and it's really just cold.
That snuggle up feeling, a soft cozy hug,
Turns a tad prickly with each frozen shrug.

Hot chocolate's a dream, till you spill it at night,
Now my shirt's a canvas, oh what a fright!
The flakes may fall soft, but the chill's got a bite,
As I shiver and grin, in this frosty light.

Glacial Isolation

Frozen in place like a statue of ice,
Waiting for warmth, oh it sure sounds nice.
My friends are all busy, no calls, what a bummer,
Guess I'll just chat with this snow-covered stumper.

The birds chirp away, but they're flying so far,
While I sit and wonder if I once had a car.
The cold's got me wrapped in a frosty embrace,
Daydreaming of sunshine in this snowbound space.

Chilling Reflections

In the fridge, where veggies freeze,
A dance of frost, a cool tease.
Penguins slip in tuxes so neat,
While snowmen have a frosty seat.

Chillin' with my frosty friends,
Making jokes that never end.
Hot cocoa sighs with dreamy steam,
Who knew winter could be a dream?

A World Built on Snow

Fortresses of snow stacked so high,
Even the squirrels pause and sigh.
Icicles hang, a pointy brigade,
Nature's way of throwing shade.

Snowball fights like cannon fire,
A winter tale we all conspire.
Hot chocolate spills on chilly hands,
A season of laughter, it never ends.

Shards of Winter's Grasp

Frosty shards in the morning glow,
They twinkle and jingle, stealing the show.
Slipping and sliding, oh what a sight,
Even the dogs are lost in delight.

Snowflakes fall like glittery dreams,
Funny old hats with quirky seams.
Bundled up tight, but what a fuss,
Who knew layering could be so robust?

Bound in Ice

Laughter echoes on frozen ponds,
Skaters slip in their speedy fronds.
A dance that spins, with quite a flair,
Chasing friends with snow in the air.

Chilly whispers tease our cheeks,
While snowmen share their frozen tweaks.
Wobbling giggles turn into cheer,
Oh winter time, we hold you dear!

Lost in Time

Days feel longer under the frost,
When digits freeze, we can't keep count.
Winter's magic slows the clock,
A playful pause in every block.

With snowflakes spun like fairy tales,
Even the sun can't break our gales.
A winter wonder where laughter blooms,
Lost in the fun amidst chilly rooms.

Frigid Hearts

In the land where penguins dance,
Hearts may freeze without a chance.
Laughter echoes through the night,
But warmth is nowhere in sight.

Snowmen wear a cheerful grin,
While frostbite starts to creep in.
No hot cocoa to be found,
Just icy jokes that spin around.

Warming Words

Chilly breezes whisper sweet,
Yet frosty tongues can't take the heat.
A joke so cold, it makes you shiver,
With punchlines that might make you quiver.

Snowflakes laugh as they fall down,
Warming words in a frosty town.
Even snowballs join the play,
As laughter melts the chill away.

Tundra's Silent Screams

The tundra's quiet, but don't be fooled,
Underneath, the ice is schooled.
Silent screams in the white expanse,
Waiting for a sunny chance.

A polar bear trips on a slick,
And laughter cracks the icy thick.
Nature's humor, white and bold,
Is really just a sight to behold.

A Glimpse Through the Ice

Looking through the frozen pane,
What a sight, what a gain!
Fish in tuxedos swim with flair,
Trying to catch the sun's warm glare.

Frosty friends in a frozen race,
Prints and giggles all embrace.
Each slip and slide, a comic show,
In this icy world, joy will flow.

Cryogenically Yours

Cryogenic dreams of delight,
Chilling ways to spend the night.
A snowball fight with a frozen twist,
Who knew cold could be such bliss?

Warm intentions lost in the freeze,
Yet giggles bounce with icy ease.
In the grip of winter's hold,
Can laughter turn the heart to gold?

Shivering Sentiments

When the chill hits hard, I start to shake,
My teeth chatter like a maraca quake.
Winter's charm has a frosty bite,
Yet I laugh as I bundle up tight.

Snowflakes fall like confetti in the air,
I sigh deeply, wishing for warmer care.
But inside my heart, I'm giggling loud,
Cold weather can never dampen this crowd.

Icy Facade

With a smile so bright, I fight the freeze,
Layers of gear, but I'm still unease.
The snowman grins, his buttons askew,
While I fumble with mittens, it's all too true.

A frosty mirror reflects my dismay,
As I slip and slide, my balance won't stay.
But laughter erupts, it's a slippery game,
This winter's stage is never the same.

The Frosted Mirror

I gaze at the glass, all fogged up and laid,
Wishing for warmth, but here I wade.
Each breath I take clouds the view,
I'm stuck in this frost, what's a girl to do?

Reflections dance in a shimmery freeze,
A portrait of chaos, yet it brings me ease.
Tinsel on branches, oh what a treat,
As I shuffle through snow, with cold frozen feet.

Cold Hands, Cold Heart

With fingers so frozen, I can barely type,
Typing 'I love winter' felt just like a hype.
But my heart's got warmth that I can ignite,
In this frosty madness, we can unite.

Chattering folks with noses so red,
Blasting joy out of snowflakes instead.
Winter rambunctious, let's have our fun,
With chilly exuberance, we all will run!

Shimmering Yet Shattered

A glint of frost, oh how it gleams,
But watch your step, it's not what it seems!
The beauty calls with a frozen smile,
One slip and down, it's quite the trial.

Snowflakes dance, a splendid show,
Yet beneath the surface, there's trouble below.
With laughter and slips, we tumble right in,
Embracing the chaos, where fun begins.

Veiled in Frost

A chill in the air, but hearts feel warm,
Bundled in layers, we weather the storm.
With frosted windows, we play peek-a-boo,
Giggling softly as the frost bites too.

Snowmen rise with a cheeky grin,
While shoveling snow, let the games begin!
Our noses red, like a clown's bright hue,
Winter's a jokester, but we laugh too.

Glacial Grievances

When mistletoe hangs, there's hugs all around,
But icy sidewalks? A perilous ground!
We waddle like penguins, oh what a sight,
In this frosty battle, we put up a fight.

Sledding with grace, or so we intend,
Until we faceplant, and laughter won't end.
Wrapped in our scarves, we snicker and tease,
Frostbitten fingers can't stop the freeze!

The Winter's Grip

A winter's grip, it cuddles us tight,
While secretly plotting a slippery plight.
Our cheeks rosy red, our spirits so high,
We leap with pure joy, then slide and we cry!

Hot cocoa awaits at the end of the race,
But first, let's conquer this icy embrace.
With cold noses and laughter, we twirl and we spin,
In the frosty chaos, let the fun begin!

Chill of the Frosty Heart

In a world of frozen glares,
Where hearts are dressed in layers,
You'd think they'd warm up quick,
But they just act like pricks.

Snowflakes dance like they own the street,
While penguins waddle on frozen feet,
They laugh at dreams of thawed delight,
But keep the hot cocoa out of sight.

Glacial Whispers

The wind whispers tales of cold,
Where warmth is deemed too bold,
Snowmen grinning, the cheeky cheats,
Throwing snowballs with frosty feats.

A squirrel dressed in snow-white fluff,
Thinks he's suave, oh so tough,
But slips and slides with frosty flair,
As laughter twinkles in the air.

The Shattered Winter Dream

Once I dreamed of snowflakes bright,
But fell flat like a snowball fight,
Chasing chill without a care,
While frostbite bites and gets unfair.

Winter's game is all a jest,
With icy jokes put to the test,
We shiver through the cold parade,
With laughter's glow, the plans we've made.

Frostbitten Echoes

They say the chill brings cozy nights,
But all I get are frosty fights,
With a mug that's empty and a tease,
Winter's here, I beg for ease.

Frozen toes and chilly cheeks,
The playful frost is full of squeaks,
Jokes that freeze before they land,
In this kingdom of ice, I stand.

The Frozen Path Beneath

Who took my slippers? Where's my shoe?
It's buried in frost, what a lovely view.
Slipping and sliding, it's a frosty dance,
I'd better be careful, give my back a chance.

Snowmen are plotting, I swear they're alive,
With noses of carrots, they seem to connive.
They wink when I trip, how dare they delight?
I'm calling a tow truck, someone help me tonight.

Glimmer of Cold Intentions

There's a glimmer of mischief, under the snow,
That ice on the sidewalk, just won't let go.
With every step taken, it's a game to the end,
I laugh as I slide, my poor shoes just bend.

Hot cocoa is glaring, from the counter so near,
But first, I must fish out, my pride from the pier.
When winter's a prankster, who would ever guess,
That laughter and falling could fall in one mess?

The Heavy Silence of Snow

The weight of white blankets, it's silent but loud,
Each flake is a giggle, beneath winter's shroud.
My cheeks get pinker, from laughs and from cold,
As nature's prankster, her mysteries unfold.

Yet behind every snowman, a joke's on the rise,
With snowballs in hand, oh they plot and they devise.
Watch out for the flurries, they're aiming for fun,
When snow's in the air, not all battles are won.

Shadows in the Frost

In shadows of twilight, the frost starts to creep,
Where snowflakes have gathered, and giggles run deep.
I bounce on my sled, it's a slippery ride,
With friends all around, there's no place to hide.

The air is electric, with jests in the night,
What's colder than winter? A friend who can bite.
So steer clear of the snowball, or dodge with some flair,
In this winter wonder, beware of the dare!

Echoes in the Glacier

Chilly winds are whipping by,
Penguins slide and laugh, oh my!
Snowflakes dance, a frosty waltz,
With every slip, they proudly vault.

Crystals spark in winter's glare,
Sledding down without a care.
Everyone is wrapped up tight,
Except that one with shorts—what's right?

Smiles freeze on faces bright,
Hot cocoa spills, oh what a sight!
Laughter echoes through the air,
As snowmen ask for extra hair.

Oh, the thrill of winter play,
Mittens lost, come what may.
A frosty world, both fun and wide,
In chilly chaos, we all slide.

Frosty Emotions Unraveled

Polar bears are taking bets,
On who slips and who forgets.
Snowball fights and snowy thrills,
Sledding down the icy hills.

Snowflakes fall like tiny stars,
Until they end up in our cars.
Jokes are tossed like snowballs too,
Laughter mixed with cold's debut.

Hot cocoa warms our frigid hands,
While icy pranks create demands.
Frosted hair and rosy cheeks,
It's the winter's playtime peaks.

In this freeze, we find our glee,
Wrapped in a blanket, just you and me.
Frosty moments, bright and fun,
Living winter, oh what a run!

Beyond the Ice Shelf

Skating on a frozen lake,
Every slip is quite the shake.
Funny faces as we fall,
Huddled close, we laugh it all.

Chilly air, it's quite the tease,
Building snowmen with such ease.
Carrot noses, hats askew,
Who knew snow could fit a shoe?

Snowflakes tickle as they land,
We play tag, a frosty band.
Hats are flying, scarves take flight,
Winter's dance is pure delight.

Underneath the winter sun,
Funny moments, never done.
Beyond the ice, we're warm inside,
In this frosty joy, we glide.

The Heart Under a Frost

Winter's chill beneath my coat,
Snowflakes drift, oh what a moat!
Under layers, laughs can freeze,
Tickling toes with icy breeze.

A snowman's smile, oh what a thrill,
As we cling to every chill.
Frostbite's threat won't stop our fun,
Plays in snow, till day is done.

The icy path, a slick delight,
Wipeouts turn to purest flight.
Everyone's a graceful elf,
Wishing they could hide themselves.

Under frozen moonlit skies,
Our laughter turns to frosty sighs.
With hearts aglow amidst the frost,
It's the silly joys we love the most.

Shimmering Illusions

In the land where frostflakes dance,
I stumbled in a fateful prance.
With a slip and a slide, oh what a show,
My legs took flight, my face said no!

I tried to skate like a pro on thin air,
But gravity had a grudge, that's not fair.
The mirror-like floor said, "Come on and glide!"
But I ended up sprawled, with nowhere to hide.

My friends all rolled with laughter so bright,
As I flailed like a fish in the failing light.
Snowballs flew with judgment so keen,
While I plotted revenge on this icy scene.

Caution: Slippery Terrain

Watch your step, it's a frosty delight,
A few hearty souls found it quite a fright.
With every bold move, you could hear the crunch,
As winter's grip gave our toes a punch.

One brave friend dared to take a leap,
But the ground became slick, and down he did creep.
With arms windmilling like a bird in flight,
He became one with the snow, what a sight!

Hot cocoa warned, stay inside please,
As the ice capades brought us to our knees.
We learned that adventure can quickly go wrong,
When you become a feature in nature's slapstick song.

The Frosted Vein

A frosty breeze with a wink and a tease,
Brought cheeky grins and chilled allergies.
With snowflakes falling like confetti of doom,
I took a step, but oh, the boom!

My boots betrayed me—it was an icy trap,
I flew like a rocket, then landed with a clap.
The ground giggled softly at my little fall,
While I rugged up, and gave it my all.

We built a fortress of pure, frozen fun,
But swift winds came, and it came undone.
With snowmen toppling and laughter galore,
This freezing escapade was hard to ignore.

Tundra's Heartache

Oh, the tundra sings a chill song so sweet,
But one wrong turn, and you're off your feet.
With a slip on the shimmer, my hopes took a dive,
As the ice turned my laughter to a gasp to survive.

A snowball duel broke out with a laugh,
As friends launched icy missiles, oh what a gaffe!
But one rogue throw went straight for my nose,
And the icy surprise made my face freeze and doze.

We learned that winter holds secrets so sly,
Like breakneck thrills and a giggling cry.
There's beauty in blunder, oh how we rejoice,
At every frosty fall—we had no choice!

Frostbitten Romance

Our love was once a fire, bright,
Now it's snowflakes in the night.
You said you'd bring the heat, my dear,
But now I'm wishing for a beer.

You took me ice skating on the pond,
Then slipped and made me look quite blonde.
A tumble here, a fall over there,
Perhaps love's warmer in the chair.

We cuddled close, beneath the stars,
But frostbite got us both with scars.
Romance was sweet, now it's a chill,
Next time I'll bring my thermal thrill.

Once soft whispers turned to shouts,
Now I'm warming up with doubts.
You're chilly, dear, so here's the deal:
I'll take hot cocoa, you just heal.

The Shiver of Regret

Under blankets, snug and warm,
I thought your heart would not alarm.
But when we danced, you took a dive,
Now we're shivering, barely alive.

You wore those boots, all shiny and new,
But slipped on ice, my laughter flew.
Now I regret that wild embrace,
You're a snowman with a frozen face.

Our warm chats turned into cold stares,
Snowflakes gather as love wears.
Every time I think of you,
I wish I'd brought a thermal shoe.

We could have ruled the winter night,
But now it's frosty, what a sight!
Next time I'll keep my distance, my friend,
For warmth and fun must surely blend.

Cold Comfort

Your hugs were once like warmth in June,
Now they give off a frosty tune.
You said our love would never freeze,
But here we are, like two cold peas.

Wrapped in layers, thick as cake,
Each time you touch, I feel a quake.
I thought your heart was bold and bright,
Now it's colder than the moonlight.

Let's build a fire, or so I say,
But you just pout and walk away.
Cold comfort's got me feeling blue,
Next time, I hope it feels like glue.

We could mix warmth with our laughter,
But ice cream's all that we get after.
So let's break out the sweat and cheer,
Before our love becomes a spear.

Crystalized Lies

You whispered sweet nothings, oh so slick,
But every promise turned to a trick.
Thought we'd fly with passion and pride,
But now I'm freezing, what a ride.

Your smile was bright, like the sun's warm rays,
Now it's crystal clear, just frozen plays.
Once melted hearts in summer glow,
Now stuck in snow, we're moving slow.

You said forever, I believed the tale,
But now I'm lost in a chilly gale.
Every glimmer turned to frost,
This love's a frosty treasure lost.

Chasing dreams in winter's white,
But found regrets that bite and bite.
Next time bring a shovel, my dear,
To dig us out from all this fear.

Glacial Shadows

In the shimmering cold, where penguins slide,
A snowman chuckles, but he's just a guise.
With snowball fights that never get old,
We laugh at the frost, we're daring and bold.

Underneath the stars, the chill's so bright,
Hot cocoa spills, oh what a sight!
Yet someone's slipping, down they go,
A frosty dance, but no one knows.

Icicles hang, like daggers of blame,
Snowflakes giggle, it's all just a game.
With frosty breath, we play silly pranks,
In glacial shadows, we form our ranks.

As the daylight fades, the chill sets in,
We wrap up warm, tuck our toes with a grin.
Though winter's here, we revel and tease,
In this frosty world, we do as we please.

Beneath the Frozen Veil

Beneath a cover of frosty delight,
Puns about snowballs, a comical sight.
The chill wraps around like a sneaky thief,
Winter's nonsense brings nothing but grief.

Mittens mismatched like a jester's attire,
We stumble and giggle, but never tire.
In frozen realms, we skate and we slide,
Oh, the snowy frolics we just can't hide.

Snowplows drift by, festive and loud,
While yelling at kids, we feel so proud.
The frozen veil hides laughter so bold,
With tales of blunders, forever retold.

Under the moon with snow so sublime,
We frolic in laughter, losing all time.
Though winter's a mess of giggles and chills,
There's warmth in the fun, and laughter fulfills.

The Frost's Bitter Embrace

The frost creeps in with a laugh and a shove,
Wrapping the world in a chilly glove.
We dance through puddles that turned into ice,
Slipping and sliding, we pay the price.

Mittens thrown high, a snowball attack,
Dodging the cold, no time to hold back.
With frosty fingers and rosy cheeks,
We build our dreams on the winter peaks.

A snowman winks, his carrot a faux,
While squirrels chatter, working for dough.
In bitter embrace, the fun never ends,
We cuddle and giggle, best of friends.

Though winter may chill, it can't freeze our glee,
For laughter is warm and sets spirits free.
So bring on the snow, we'll dance through the night,
With joyous abandon, everything's right.

Shattered Dreams of Winter

In winter's realm where dreams turn to ice,
We trip over snowmen; oh, isn't it nice?
Laughs fill the air as we tumble around,
With shattered hopes lying flat on the ground.

Sweaters so chunky, we waddle with flair,
Giggling with joy as we fall through the air.
In-harmonious jingles, our skates clash and glide,
With each frosty plunge, there's nowhere to hide.

The snowflakes tease; they giggle and stand,
As we flail through winter, no plans ever grand.
Yet life's frosty gaffes make stories worth telling,
In the heart of the blizzard, our laughter is swelling.

From snowball battles to sledding down hills,
Each frozen disaster, a memory that thrills.
So let's raise a glass to the shivers and fun,
With frostbitten toes, we'll laugh till we're done.

Glare of the Icy Realm

In the grip of winter's glee,
Frostbitten toes revolt in me.
Snowmen laughing, their noses bright,
Yet my cocoa's freezing overnight.

Slippery sidewalks, a dance of doom,
Falling flat on my living room.
Neighbors chuckle, the cats conspire,
While I contemplate my warmest attire.

Icicles hanging in a festive line,
Candy canes that never taste fine.
I tried to sled, but oh dear me,
The hill was a mountain; it set me free!

With laughter echoing at every turn,
In this icy realm, I live and learn.
So here's to winter, with all its flares,
In the land of frost, no one really cares.

Winter's Cruel Caress

Shivers lurking in the breeze,
I bundled up, but still it teases.
My hand's a popsicle, this can't be right,
Dancing snowflakes laugh at my plight.

Furries prancing in fluffy coats,
While I search for my lost winter notes.
A snowball fight? Oh what a jest,
With icy traps that leave me depressed.

Hot chocolate's warmth turns cold and stale,
As mugs slip from my frozen trail.
Winter's embrace, a cold surprise,
Turning my nose to frosty fries.

Yet here I stand, a merry fool,
Wrapped in layers, a winter tool.
Through snowy laughter, I find delight,
In winter's grip, a silly fight.

Beneath a Shroud of Snow

Covered in white like a flaky pie,
The world looks soft, but oh me, oh my!
Underneath, the ice hides many a tale,
Of slips and trips that never fail.

Sledding down lanes like a bird on a wire,
A journey that lands me right in the mire.
With boots like anchors sunk deep in snow,
Finding my feet is a day-long show.

Frosty windows, a canvas of cheer,
Skaters twirling, but I still steer clear.
The frozen pond looks smooth as glass,
But one wrong step? Oh, what a gas!

Yet laughter rides on each chilly gust,
As sounds of joy give winter its thrust.
Under this shroud of snowy cheer,
We waddle and giggle, full of good cheer.

The Chill of Betrayal

Betrayed by the frost, where did it all go?
I wanted winter, not a frozen show.
Shrunken snowsuits hug like a vice,
As I plan my escape, oh, isn't it nice?

Betrayal's sweet scent of peppermint dreams,
Now masked by the chill and busted seams.
My snow angel flops, a desperate attempt,
In this winter wonder, I feel quite unkempt.

Frosted windows hide the truth within,
The weather's fine, but I'm feeling thin.
Jokes on me as I slip and slide,
Wishing for warmth as I bide my pride.

Yet amid the cold, I laugh with glee,
For winter's grip is a sight to see.
Betrayal, you frosty, you comedic beast,
In this icebox joke, I'm never the least.

A Winter's Tale Untold

Snowflakes dance in moonlit night,
Frosty whispers, such delight.
Sleds are racing down the hill,
Can we take a moment, still?

Gloves mismatched, style still bright,
Falling down, a comical sight.
Hot cocoa spills, laughter reigns,
Winter antics, joy unchains.

The snowman wobbles, nose askew,
A carrot thief? Oh, what a view!
He melts away, the sun's embrace,
But memories leave a lasting trace.

Our laughter echoes, crisp and clear,
Winter's whims, we hold them dear.
Through frosted panes, we peek outside,
A frosty world, our hearts abide.

Hidden Truths in the Snow

Underneath the blinding white,
Secrets buried out of sight.
Snowball fights and playful toss,
Whispers lost in wintry gloss.

Footprints lead to mystery,
Did she fall, or climb a tree?
The dog's delight, he hops and bounds,
Catching flakes that swirl around.

Frozen puddles, slippery fate,
Down we go, it's not too late!
Laughter echoes through the chill,
Who knew snow could bring such thrill?

Hidden truths in every flake,
Joyful moments, memories make.
As we gather, hot drinks in hand,
Winter's wonders, oh so grand.

The Shivering Heart's Lament

Beneath the quilt of snow so frigid,
My heart's a block, feeling rigid.
Chilly breezes, shivers start,
Why can't winter warm the heart?

Frosty mornings, coffee's bliss,
But every sip feels like a miss.
The sun peeks out but plays coy,
Chasing warmth, a timid joy.

In huddled coats, we walk in lines,
Jokes on lips, warmth in signs.
Yet frozen feet and noses red,
Giggles bubble, laughter spread.

A shivering heart across this land,
Funny moments, warming hand.
Winter's grip may cause us dread,
But love and laughter break the thread.

Echoes of a Bitter Chill

Whispering winds, a chilly face,
Slip and slide, we join the race.
Frosty bites, oh what a groove,
In this dance, we can't improve.

Scarves wrapped tight, hats a bit askew,
Chatter and chuckles, old and new.
Let's not take ourselves too serious,
This winter wonderland, delirious.

Icicles dangle, a pointy threat,
But watch your head, don't place your bet!
With every slip, a lesson learned,
Winter's chill can leave us turned.

Echoes of laughter fill the air,
In frozen moments, joy we share.
With each chill, a story spun,
In this winter, we find our fun.

The Frigid Edge of Reality

In winter's clutches, we all slide,
Be careful, slippery paths abide.
With snowball fights that break the norm,
Laughter echoes; hurt feelings, warm.

Frosty breath in the icy air,
I trip and tumble, land in despair.
A penguin waddle, arms spread wide,
Laughing so hard, I can't seem to hide.

Jackets bundled, too few mittens,
Socks dampened; oh, my poor kittens!
Each frosty gust, it gives a laugh,
How can one fall and then take a bath?

Yet through the chill, joy takes its stance,
In frozen chaos, we find our dance.
The frigid edge, a slippery page,
Life's winter tales, our stage, most sage.

Echos Beneath the Ice

Under the frost, secrets lay deep,
Thoughts arise like dreams we keep.
Whispers of penguins all around,
Cracks in the ice, let laughter resound.

Slipping and sliding, we forge ahead,
What lies beneath? Sweet dreams or dread?
Yet giggles spill from the frozen plight,
Turns out, tripping is pure delight.

Snow angels made with a playful flair,
Snowmen shaped with a comical air.
With icy jokes, we share the fun,
Underneath this wintry sun.

Though chilly winds might knock us down,
In frozen humor, we hold our crown.
With every slip, we rise in stride,
In this icy world, we safely glide.

Crystalline Memories

Reflective shards in the sun's bright sheen,
Glimmers of laughter, a playful scene.
Memories freeze, like moments caught,
In the chill of time, joy is sought.

A snowball flies, it finds a face,
Who's heaving now, what a funny grace!
Kids and adults are all in the fray,
Who knew that winter could be this play?

Beneath the cold, smiles never dwindle,
Each icy fall, sharp as a spindle.
The crunch of snow breaks the silent night,
Echoes of laughter take flight in white.

Frosty reminders warm up the soul,
Each crystalline fragment makes me whole.
In this frozen space, let joy arise,
With memories bright as the winter skies.

The Chilling Dance of Shadows

The shadows flicker, they sway and glide,
Like playful dancers, they twist and slide.
With goofy moves, they steal the show,
In the winter's chill, we all let go.

Snowflakes tumble, each one unique,
A frosty pirouette, nothing bleak.
In the moonlight, we cha-cha with flair,
Tripping and laughing, without a care.

The cool night calls with a cheeky grin,
Embrace the chill, let the fun begin.
With icy feet and spirits bright,
We dance away into the night.

So join the party, ignore the cold,
In each shadow's dance, let love unfold.
With every slip, let's twirl and sway,
In this winter waltz that lasts all day.

Frost Crystals on Whispered Lies

Frosty whispers dance and gleam,
Secrets wrapped in a frosty theme.
Snowflakes giggle, mischievous they glide,
While frosted truths try to hide.

Chilly thoughts in a winter's breath,
Silly stories, bringing us to death.
Icicles hang with a mocking tone,
Lies frozen solid, all alone.

Snowmen plotting, their carrot noses twist,
Chortling under the blizzard's mist.
Cold air crackles, the humor's bold,
Here lies the laughter in a world so cold.

Jokesters lurking, snowballs in tow,
A frosty prank that steals the show.
Under ice, a chuckle grows loud,
In this winter, we're all foolishly proud.

Paralyzing Cold

A chill so deep, you freeze in place,
Teeth clattering, what a funny face!
Frostbite grips with a playful tease,
Fingers numb, but still we sneeze.

Laughter echoes in a frozen land,
Hilarious slips, accidents unplanned.
Sledding fails, down the hill we crash,
Winter's comedy in a frosty splash.

Hot cocoa warms, but not the toes,
Jumping up and down, a silly show.
Shivering giggles fill the air,
Who knew cold would make us care?

A polar dance, with flailing charms,
Frosty as a snowman's arms.
In this freeze, our spirits lift,
Laughter's a present, winter's gift.

Tides of Coldness

Waves of frost crash on the shore,
Chilly giggles, we laugh for more.
Sandy snowflakes swirl all around,
In this icy tide, joy is found.

Surfing on snow, what a quirky dream,
Sliding and gliding, we're part of the scheme.
Snowmen catching waves in the glow,
Riding frosty laughter, go with the flow!

Seas of winter in a playful fling,
Tickled by breezes, hear the frost sing.
Frozen toes dance on icy earth,
As laughter splashes, it's winter's mirth.

Crystals twinkle like stars in the night,
Clumsy snowball fights bring pure delight.
With icy grins on our frozen faces,
We ride the tide to hilarious places.

The Silent Scream of Frost

Beneath the freeze, a silent moan,
Frozen grins, we've turned to stone.
Chilly shadows creep and crawl,
While laughter echoes through winter's hall.

Huddled tight, we share our woes,
But underneath, the humor flows.
Noses redder than Rudolph's fame,
In the cold, we're all the same.

Teeth chatter in the frosty breeze,
Trying not to shiver, oh please!
Frosty breath makes laughter bolder,
While winter wraps its chilly shoulder.

Loud cackles through the shivering night,
In this frosted world, everything's light.
As winter whispers, "Let's share a chill,"
We scream with joy, while time stands still.

Beneath the Frozen Surface

In a land where snowmen roam,
Glittering chill, but not a home.
Every penguin wears a frown,
Sipping cocoa upside down.

Frosty feet in frozen boots,
Waddling past the runaway moose.
Laughter echoes with a twist,
In a snowball fight, who'd resist?

Under layers, warmth's disguise,
Feeling chilly, oh what a surprise!
Hot cocoa spills, laughter's plight,
Chasing snowflakes in the night.

Snowflakes melt, the party ends,
Chattering teeth, just like old friends.
We'll dance and spin, lose all our cares,
When spring arrives, who still prepares?

The Frosty Facade

Behind a smile, winter grins,
With a snowball, let the fun begin!
Chilly cheeks and frosty hair,
But slipping on ice? Let's not go there!

Gale force winds, a wild breeze,
Twirling round like autumn leaves.
Everyone's sliding, oh what a sight,
Laughs are plenty, fears take flight.

Pine trees dressed in white and gold,
Tales of frostbite, yet we are bold.
With every sigh, a gust of air,
Who knew winter could be quite rare?

The snowman looks, just like the king,
As kids throw snow, they laugh and sing.
But deep inside, the truth is near,
Funny how cold can bring such cheer!

A Dance with the Ice Queen

The queen of chill with fingers light,
Leads us through a waltz so tight.
With every step, we bear the cold,
But who could dance when tales unfold?

Her icy crown's a shimmery sight,
With a wink she turns, makes it bright.
Slipping and sliding, we spin around,
Yet clumsy feet bring laughter sound.

She twirls with grace on frostbit ground,
While students tumble, laughter's found.
An icy breath, a frozen shout,
In this ballet, no want to pout!

As the music plays, we adhere,
To the frosty rhythm, casting fear.
With each misstep, the fun draws near,
It's not about grace, but joy we steer!

Winter's Lament

Oh winter, dear, you take your toll,
With frozen fingers, you're on a roll.
The shivers come, all dressed in white,
But under that snow, we're ready to fight.

Lamenting greets a chilly morn,
While every breath sounds like a horn.
The roads are slick, yet smile resumes,
With capers, slips, and belly flumes.

Hot cider warms our sinking hearts,
As ice-princess plays in frozen arts.
Snowflakes fall, a jolly crew,
But be careful where you step, that's true!

So here's to laughs in winter's game,
Slipping, sliding, we'll stake our claim.
Though cold may bite with teeth so sharp,
We'll freeze the night with warmth and spark!

Shards of a Frozen Heart

In a world so cold, I trip and slide,
My heart's made of shards, I just can't hide.
With jokes on my lips, I'm wrapped in a freeze,
Laughing through frosts, like it's all just a tease.

Fingers turn blue, but I still can joke,
With snowflakes as buddies, I play like a bloke.
The chill's not so bad when you're cracking a grin,
With every slip-up, let the fun begin.

Penguin-waddle, I try to get near,
But my frozen demeanor gives everyone fear.
A dance on the ice, a frosty ballet,
Giggling at shadows, who really needs rays?

So grab me a hot drink, make it quite sweet,
We'll toast to the chill with cold, happy feet.
A heart made of glass may be hard to break,
But with laughter abound, there's no frost to shake.

Subzero Serenade

When temperatures drop, I break into song,
A tune of mishaps, where everyone's wrong.
With snow in my hair and a grin on my face,
   I croon to the stars in this frozen place.

The winter will shake, I'll giggle and cry,
   As I slip on the ice—oh my! Oh my!
With mittens too small and boots tied too tight,
I serenade shadows in the moonlight bright.

Frosty the snowman, he's my partner in crime,
As we bumble through snowdrifts, out of our rhyme.
Singing to neighbors with cookies that dropped,
I serve up the laugh, though the oven just flopped.

So bring out the warmth, let's dance on this freeze,
With jokes as our jackets, we'll do as we please.
A comic upheaval in a wintery show,
   Subzero serenades, oh what a fun flow!

Crystalized Shadows

In glimmers and sparkles, my shadow does dance,
With each step I take, I lose my balance.
I trip over laughter, my face is aglow,
As winter's cold grip takes the center stage show.

The frost clings like glitter, so sparkly and bright,
But in icy corners, things sneak out of sight.
I chuckle at snowmen with hats slightly askew,
Their crooked little shirts give them humor anew.

Behind every white wall, a secret does hide,
A tumble, a slip, and my pride is denied.
The crystals may twinkle, but warmth starts to flare,
As we roll like snowballs, without any care.

With giggles and gaffes, we fashion a tale,
In a world of cold whispers, our laughter won't pale.
Crystalized shadows on this playful spree,
In a frostbitten saga, let's all just be free!

When Warmth Turns to Chill

Once basking in sunshine, now lost in a freeze,
Chirps of the summer seem petty like fleas.
A scarf wrapped too tight, what has become real?
The warmth drips away with each shivering squeal.

I wish for a coconut, under the sun,
But here I am, slipping, oh look, it's begun!
Snowmen are laughing and so are the trees,
While I prance through the tundra with frozen knees.

In snowball fights started, intentions run high,
Yet frosty surprise leaves my ego awry.
When warmth is a whisper and chill fills the air,
I'll skip through the tundra with not a care.

So here's to the winter, a season of fun,
With giggles and frost, let's shine like the sun.
With puns in the air, we'll take every spill,
As we dance through the chill, yes, let's take that thrill!

A Caress of Winter's Sting

Winter dances, a frosty strut,
Snowflakes twirl, a chilly glut.
Laughing loudly, the cold winds blow,
Bundled up, we put on a show.

Hot cocoa warms, though it's a tease,
Every sip brings a chill with ease.
Frosty jokes fly, they drift and slip,
In this season, we've got the grip.

Sleds zip down with gleeful squeals,
Who knew winter had such great appeals?
Each frozen puddle a slippery prank,
Just when we think we've got our rank.

So let us laugh at the cold's embrace,
While twirling and spinning in frosty space.
With winter's touch, our giggles grow,
A caress of frost, with a silly glow.

Shadows in the Crystal Cold

Outdoors we play, shadows perform,
In a tangle of winter, a comical swarm.
Footprints vanish, then suddenly slide,
On frozen ground, there's nowhere to hide.

Snowmen grinning, a silly parade,
Mittens shaking, mischief displayed.
Throwing snowballs, we aim and miss,
Winter's a jester, we share a bliss.

Hot noses and cheeks, all bright and red,
Frosty puns dance in our winter bed.
Under the stars, the night sparkles clear,
We chuckle together, banishing fear.

With each gust of wind, a playful shout,
Winter's not so serious, that's what it's about.
We'll laugh at the chill, take it in stride,
In shadows of crystal, our hearts open wide.

Chill in the Air

A dreadfully funny chill in the air,
All bundled up, we dance without care.
Frosty breath hangs, like whispers of glee,
In layers of sweaters, we're wild and free.

Skipping through snow, oh what a sight,
The ground may be slippery, but spirits are bright.
Falling and laughing, we tumble and roll,
With winter gold dust, filling our soul.

Noses turn pink, cheeks glow with the fun,
The cold wraps around us, but here comes the sun.
Sipping hot drinks, we warm up with cheer,
Joking and jabbing, forgetting the fear.

So here's to the chill, let laughter ring loud,
In winter's embrace, we're all feeling proud.
With joy and with jokes, we'll conquer the cold,
Through laughter we find, like treasures, we hold.

Frosted Whispers

Frosted whispers in the wild night air,
Giggling at snowflakes that drift without care.
Bundled tight in our colorful fluff,
Our cheeks like apples, winter's no bluff.

We trip on icicles, dance on the frost,
Turning these blunders into laughter embossed.
Through snowball battles, we gleefully brawl,
Each frosty encounter, we're having a ball.

Snow-laden branches all droop with delight,
Nature's own humor, it's a magical sight.
As icicles tinkle and twinkle like stars,
Funny memories echo, they're never too far.

Wrap up this season, with hugs nice and tight,
In the midst of cold, we create our own light.
These frosted whispers, we'll cherish and keep,
When winter concludes, in laughter we leap.

Milton Keynes UK
Ingram Content Group UK Ltd.
UKHW022341171124
451242UK00007B/80